KU-351-242

Contents

Published in 1982 by Kingfisher Books Limited,
Elsley Court, 20-22 Great Titchfield Street,
London W1 P 7AD
© Piper Books Limited 1982

All Rights Reserved

Printed by Graficas Reunidas S.A., Madrid, Spain

BRITISH LIBRARY CATALOGUING IN PUBLICATION DATA
Lambert, David
  Planet earth.—(Kingfisher factbooks; 12)
  1.   Earth—Juvenile literature
  I.   Title
  550   QE29
ISBN 0 86272 033 8

PLANET EARTH

By David Lambert

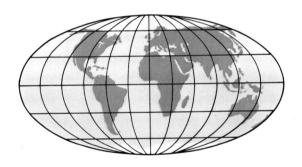

Editor: Jacqui Bailey
Series Design: David Jefferis

KINGFISHER

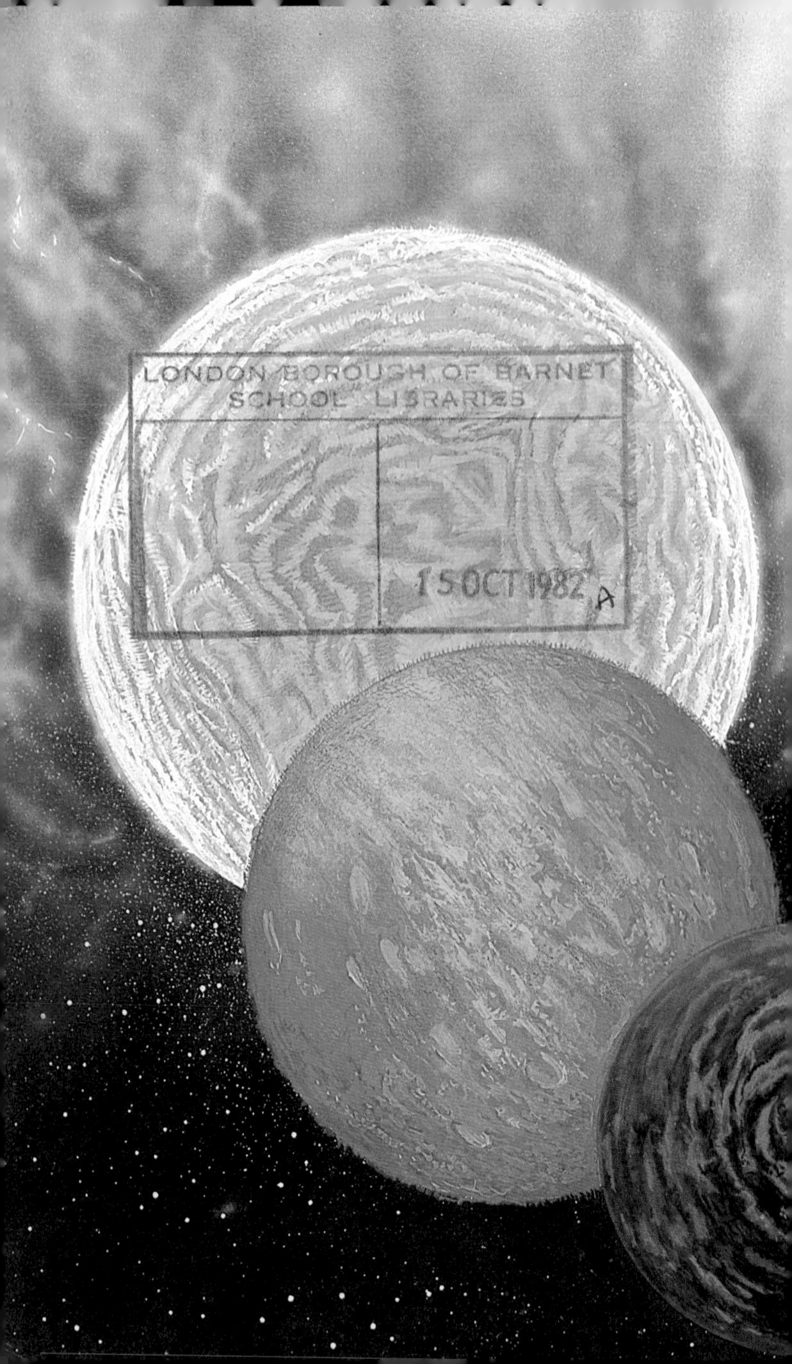

Earth in the Making

Six thousand million years ago the Earth was just a cloud of dusts and gases whirling through empty space. Bit by bit these particles pulled one another together. In time they became bits of ice and frozen gas mixed with rock and metal. The particles then resembled dirty snowflakes.

Time passed and the 'snowflakes' began to stick together to make giant 'snowballs'. Then it was their turn to stick together. By 4600 million years ago they formed one mighty ball—the planet Earth.

Earth's Crust Takes Shape

As the Earth's ingredients squashed together they gave off immense heat. This melted the inside of the Earth. Its heavy ingredients sank to the centre and lighter ones rose to the surface. Some floated like a scum and formed a crust. The young crust shook, and leaked molten rock on to a surface that was airless, waterless and baking hot.

Water trapped inside the hot Earth became steam. This, and other hot gases, escaped from the crust to form the Earth's first atmosphere. As the crust cooled and hardened, rains fell. This great deluge continued for millions of years and slowly the seas filled huge dips in the crust. The continents and oceans began to appear.

The Earth in Space

The Earth is only one of nine planets that loop around a great ball of white-hot gas much larger than themselves. This fiery ball is the star we call the Sun.

The Sun, its planets and their moons form one mighty solar system. Yet this great group is just a speck among the 100,000 million stars that form the star group that people call the Milky Way.

The Sun is the only star near enough to the Earth to affect what happens here. The Sun's pull, called *gravitation*, stops the Earth escaping into outer space. The Sun's rays light and warm the Earth. Without them life here would be impossible.

The Earth spins once in 24 hours on an axis with its ends at the poles.

When the north pole (N) tilts towards the Sun it is summer in the northern hemisphere, winter in the south. When the Sun is directly over the equator at midday it is spring or autumn.

Days, Seasons, Years

The Earth is spinning as it travels. With each spin sunlight and darkness bring day and night. It takes a year for the Earth to orbit the Sun.

The Earth is tilted at an angle to the Sun. The seasons change as each half of the Earth tilts towards the Sun, then away. When it is winter in the north, it is summer in the south.

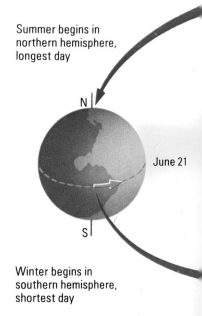

Summer begins in northern hemisphere, longest day

June 21

Winter begins in southern hemisphere, shortest day

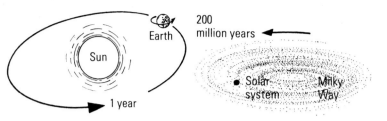

A year lasts 365¼ days, the time it takes the Earth to orbit the Sun.

Our solar system takes 200 million years to orbit the Milky Way galaxy.

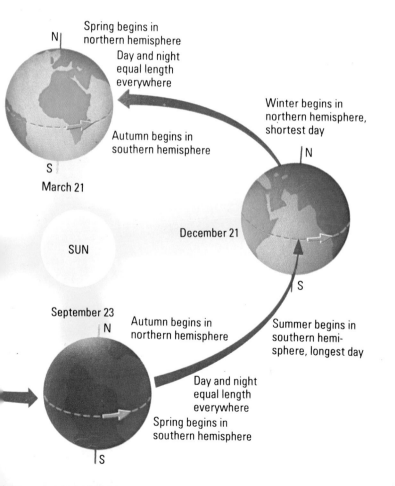

Spring begins in northern hemisphere
Day and night equal length everywhere
Autumn begins in southern hemisphere
March 21

Winter begins in northern hemisphere, shortest day

December 21

SUN

September 23
Autumn begins in northern hemisphere

Summer begins in southern hemisphere, longest day

Day and night equal length everywhere
Spring begins in southern hemisphere

Inside the Earth

We have seen our planet from space and we know much about its shape and size. We know the Earth is like a giant ball, slightly flattened at the poles and with a slight bulge at the equator. We know that a journey around the Earth would measure more than 40,000 kilometres.

We know, too, that from the Earth's surface to its middle is more than 6000 kilometres—farther than from London to New York. Yet no one has drilled deeper than ten kilometres. Down there the rocks are hotter than boiling water. But no one has ever seen the rocks that are deeper than that.

S-Waves and P-Waves
Luckily, scientists have other ways of finding out about the Earth's interior. They study the effects of earthquakes and man-made explosions. Both send shock waves through the planet. The so-called S-waves only pass through solid substances. P-waves pass through solids or liquids. Both waves move at different speeds through different substances.

Scientists measured how long it took different waves to reach different places on the Earth's surface. This showed them that the Earth's inside is made up of several layers.

The Layered Earth
The four main layers of the Earth are the crust, the

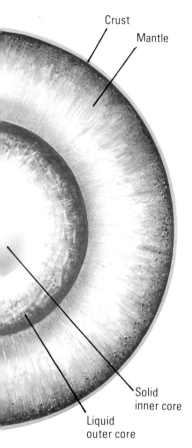

Crust

Mantle

Solid inner core

Liquid outer core

This diagram shows the Earth cut open to reveal its inside. Most of the Earth's bulk is in its inner layers: the mantle and the two-part core. Continents are just part of the thin outer crust.

layer is about 2900 kilometres thick, and very hot. Parts of the upper mantle move like sticky tar.

Below the mantle lies the outer core, an iron and nickel shell more than 2200 kilometres thick. Immense heat makes it liquid.

Lastly comes the inner core—a ball of metal about 2440 kilometres across, and even hotter than the outer core. The layers pressing on it from above help to keep the inner core solid.

A Giant Magnet

The molten metal of the outer core flows very slowly. It probably takes ten years to flow 100 kilometres. But scientists think that this is fast enough to make the core act like a dynamo, to produce electricity.

This makes the Earth behave as a giant magnet with its ends at the magnetic north and south poles, near the geographic poles. This is why compass needles point north-south.

mantle, the outer core and the inner core. The hard crust—the outer rocky layer —is the thinnest layer. The crust is about 40 kilometres thick under the continents but far thinner below the oceans.

The light rocks making up the crust float on the heavier rocks of the mantle. This

Restless Continents

Most land lies in seven mighty chunks: the continents. These are scattered round the world. But scientists think that long ago all the continents were stuck together.

Several clues show that this is likely. For instance, the east coasts of North and South America could have fitted into the west coasts of Europe and Africa. Then, too, rocks on each side of the Atlantic Ocean match one another. Even some of the plants and animals in continents now far apart share the same close ancestors.

A Shifting Jigsaw Puzzle

At first it seemed impossible that continents could drift about, but scientists have now discovered how it could happen. They believe that the continents are moved around by currents of molten rock flowing through the Earth's mantle. Rising currents bring heat up from the Earth's core. Where a rising current reaches the Earth's crust the current spreads out in opposite directions and pulls the crust apart. Then the current plugs the gap with molten rock. Where spreading currents cool they grow heavier and sink, dragging crust down into the mantle.

It seems that the Earth's crust is made up of over a dozen interlocking plates or slabs. Some of these carry ocean floor. Some carry continents. All fit like pieces of a jigsaw puzzle—but a puzzle where the pieces keep on moving.

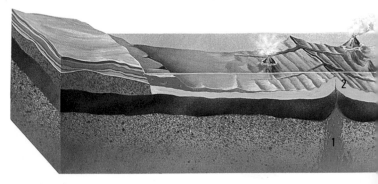

300 million years ago

135 million years ago

The world today

These world maps show how the continents may have shifted. They were all one mighty continent, known as Pangaea, 300 million years ago. By 135 million years ago this was splitting up. Now India, Antarctica, Australia and America all lie in new positions.

Below: (1) a current in the mantle rises and spreads below an ocean floor to split the crust, but molten rock wells up and builds an underwater mountain ridge (2). A cooling current sinks (3) and drags the crust into the mantle, pushing up volcanic mountains.

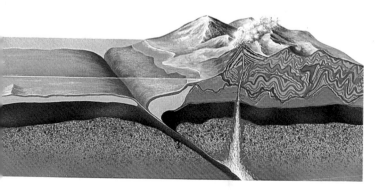

The Quaking Crust

Sometimes, two of the great plates that are part of the Earth's crust grind against each other. If one moves against another with a sudden jerk the ground above will shake. Huge cracks may open up across fields and roads. The land on one side of a crack may rise or fall, or slip sideways against the land on the far side of the crack. Buildings may sway and crash, killing people inside them.

Giant Waves

All this and more can happen in an earthquake. If the earthquake happens under the sea, huge shock waves called *tsunami* travel outward. These waves can travel at hundreds of kilometres an hour. If they enter shallow bays, tsunami may tower taller than a house and roar inland, perhaps drowning towns and villages.

Earthquake Belts

Each year special instruments help the world's scientists to detect about half a million earthquakes. Most happen where a crustal plate

overrides another or slips sideways past it.

Most earthquakes happen in belts of land from North Africa to China and round the Pacific Ocean.

Of every 500 earthquakes, only one is very damaging. The worst recent earthquake killed three-quarters of a million people in the Chinese city of T'ang-shan in 1976.

One day scientists may be able to foretell and even prevent severe earthquakes.

Below: In 1964 a severe earthquake hit Alaska, shifting ground up or down by over 15 metres.

This instrument records earth tremors as a jagged line drawn on a turning drum by a tracer hung from a spring.

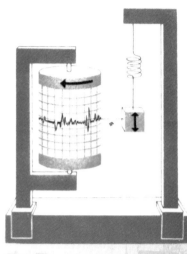

Volcanoes

In certain places around the world, molten rock from deep down in the ground leaks out through holes or cracks. These places are volcanoes. Some volcanoes are quiet, some explosive, some in between.

Quiet volcanoes gently ooze hot, runny rock. When it flows out on the surface this rock is called *lava*. Very runny lava spreads out across the surrounding land. Less runny lava builds a gently sloping cone around the hole or crater that it comes from. Sticky lava builds a tall, steep-sided cone.

Violent Volcanoes
Explosive volcanoes erupt with sudden force. Hot gas trapped underground presses on the rocks above until it hurls them from the mouth of the volcano. Hot ash, cinders and molten rock shoot up into the sky and fall back like mortar shells. Explosive volcanoes build steep cones, mainly made of thick layers of ash.

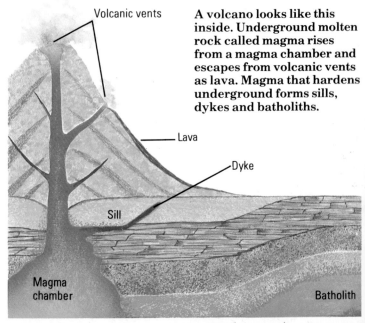

Volcanic vents

Lava

Dyke

Sill

Magma chamber

Batholith

A volcano looks like this inside. Underground molten rock called magma rises from a magma chamber and escapes from volcanic vents as lava. Magma that hardens underground forms sills, dykes and batholiths.

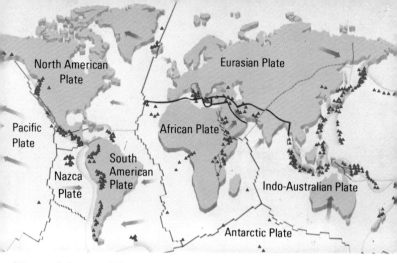

Many of the world's 455 active land volcanoes rim the Pacific Ocean where the crust is weak.

→	Direction plate is moving
—	Collision zone
▲	Volcano

A third kind of volcano sometimes quietly leaks lava, and sometimes shoots out ash and gas. Such 'in-between' volcanoes produce cones from sandwiched layers of ash and lava.

Inactive Volcanoes

In time volcanoes stop erupting. A volcano may lie quiet for centuries. But it may be merely dormant (sleeping). Hot gas could be building up below a lava plug that blocks its outlet. At last the gas pressure may suddenly blast off the volcano's lid with an immense explosion. About 1470 BC the Greek island of Santorini blew up with a force as great as that of hundreds of hydrogen bombs.

Some volcanoes stop erupting for good. Edinburgh Castle stands on the remains of one of these extinct, or dead, volcanoes.

Where Volcanoes Grow

Like earthquakes, active volcanoes occur where the Earth's crustal plates are separating or colliding. At such weak places in the Earth's crust, *magma* (molten underground rock) can well up and escape.

Building Mountains

Collisions between the great plates of the Earth's crust do more than trigger earthquakes and volcanic eruptions; they build mountains.

Earth's Tallest Peaks

About 40 million years ago India was an island slowly colliding with Asia. Between them lay a sea with a floor of layered rocks. As India and Asia collided, the sea floor was squashed and forced into huge humps called *fold mountains*. These are the Himalayas—the highest mountain range on Earth. In much the same way, the European Alps were pushed upward as Italy nosed into southern Europe.

The Alps and Himalayas belong to a great system of fold mountains stretching from Morocco to China.

The Rockies and Andes

The Rocky Mountains of western North America and the Andes of western South America form another great mountain system.

The Andes and Rockies have risen where the western edge of the Americas rides over the eastern edge of crustal plates under the Pacific Ocean. As the oceanic plates are forced down into the hot mantle, their rocks melt. But these rocks are lighter than the rocks of the mantle. So they rise back up through the mantle and then are pushed up through the crustal plates that carry North and South America (see page 13).

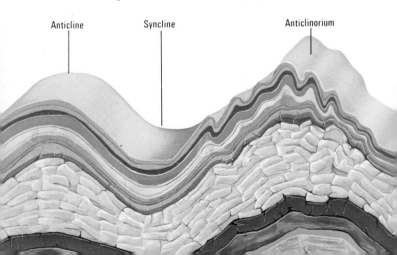

Anticline   Syncline   Anticlinorium

This is why there are so many volcanoes in western North and South America. Most of their highest mountains are volcanic.

Block Mountains

When crustal plates jostle one another great cracks, called *faults*, appear in the Earth's crust. Sometimes a block of land is squeezed up between two faults and forms a flat-topped mountain, called a *block mountain*. Europe's Vosges and Black Forest are block mountains.

Sometimes a narrow block of land sinks between two faults. The sunken land is a *rift valley*. The longest one runs through Africa.

Right: The sharply pointed Matterhorn is one of the most famous sights of the European Alps.

Shifting crustal plates may buckle rock layers (left) or move them up and down (below right).

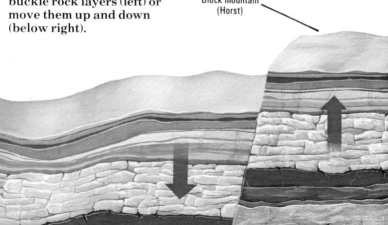

Block mountain (Horst)

How Rocks Are Made

There are many hundred kinds of rock. All come directly or indirectly from magma—the molten rock which lies beneath the hard rocks of the Earth's crust.

Fiery Rocks

'Fiery' or *igneous* rocks occur where magma has welled up, then cooled and hardened.

Sometimes it happens underground. Granite forms like this. Great blobs of granite grow like giant underground blisters that show up when the rocks above are gradually worn away.

Basalt and obsidian are igneous rocks that form when magma cools and hardens on the surface.

Granite cools so slowly its ingredients have time to form crystals big enough for us to see. Obsidian cools too fast for crystals to grow; it looks like glass.

The crystals found in rocks like granite are called *minerals*. There are more than 2000 kinds altogether.

Different minerals form at different temperatures. They 'freeze' out of magma one by one as the magma cools.

Sedimentary Rocks

Sedimentary rocks are made from loose particles (sediments) that have piled up on land or in water. The pressure of the sediments above squashes those below. Then natural cements glue the squashed sediments together to form solid rock.

Sediments and sedimentary rocks cover more than two-thirds of the Earth's surface. Some sedimentary layers are several hundred metres thick. In many places different sedimentary rocks lie on top of each other like layers in a sandwich.

Different sedimentary rocks have different ingredi-

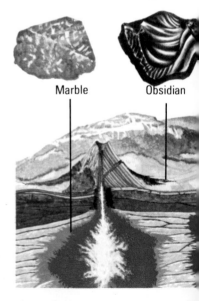

Marble

Obsidian

ents. Sandstone is often made of grains of quartz from broken down granite. Limestone comes largely from the hard shells and skeletons of billions of tiny sea animals.

Most sedimentary rocks are formed from broken down igneous rocks—they are igneous rocks at second hand.

Metamorphic Rocks

Metamorphic or 'changed form' rocks are igneous or sedimentary rocks changed into new kinds of rock by great heat or enormous pressure.

When a great mass of molten rock is pushed up through the Earth's crust it alters the rocks around it. In this way, limestone changes into marble as its shelly mass of calcium carbonate becomes hard calcite crystals.

Metamorphic rocks are also formed in the buckling that builds fold mountains. Heat changes soft mudstone into hard slate. At higher temperatures slate changes into mica-schist. If things get hotter still, mica-schist produces rock called gneiss.

Examples of the three main rock types: marble (metamorphic), obsidian and granite (igneous), limestone and conglomerate (sedimentary).

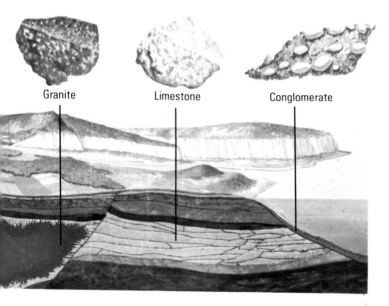

Granite   Limestone   Conglomerate

Land Under Attack

We have seen how mountains grow and rocks are made. Now we shall take a look at how the surface of the land is being worn away. This usually takes place so slowly that we do not see it happening. It can take over 12,000 years to wear away a layer of soil and rock one metre thick.

First, weather attacks the surface of the solid rock and breaks it up. Wind, rain, frost or sunshine start by seeking out any weakness in a rock. Many rocks have loose particles or cracks between their blocks or layers. They may be soft or easily dissolved by water. Weathering splits or rots rocks where they lie.

Rocks That Break with a Bang
Heating and cooling break up much of the surface rock. In hot deserts it may be hot by day but cold by night. As a rocky surface warms up it tries to stretch; as it cools down it tries to

Left: Hot days and cold nights help to split solid rock and form a mass of desert rubble.

Above: Frost-loosened flakes of rock lie in heaps on a mountainside.

Left: Limestone rocks dissolved by rain leave bare, stony surfaces.

shrink. Meanwhile, the rock below neither shrinks nor stretches. So strains occur inside the rock. As dusk falls, flakes of rock may break off from the surface with sharp sounds like gunshots.

In cool, damp climates rainwater collects in rocky crevices. On mountains the water freezes at dusk and melts at dawn. Each time the ice forms it pushes against the sides of its crevice. This splits off chunks of rock, which fall downhill and form loose heaps called *scree*.

Rocks That Turn to Powder

Some kinds of rock contain ingredients that dissolve in rain-water. When rainwater falls on them these ingredients are swept away and the rocks crumble. Limestone rock may dissolve completely (see pages 26-27). In granite, the hard felspar crystals rot to a soft, powdery clay. Without felspar to bind them, the other crystals drop out and form heaps of sand.

Surface rocks are also attacked by plants. Plants produce acids that dissolve the rock. The roots of plants invade and widen cracks. They can even shatter boulders.

Landscape features
formed by a river:
(1) V-shaped valley
(2) Waterfall
(3) Gorge
(4) Meander
(5) Ox-bow lake
(6) Flood plain
(7) Delta

Rivers at Work

Once weathering has broken up the surface rock, running water can start to carry it away. Scientists believe that rivers remove 140 tonnes of rock and soil each year from each square kilometre of land. Given long enough, rivers and the streams that feed them can wear away the highest mountain ranges.

Mountain Streams

Rivers get their water from rain that falls upon the land. In places, rain sinks down through the ground until it meets a rock layer with no holes or cracks that it can filter through. Where this layer forms part of a hillside, the water escapes by bubbling up as a spring. Many rivers start as springs on mountainsides.

Springs feed streams that flow downhill. A stream flows quickly if a mountainside is steep. The mountain stream picks up bits of rock loosened by the weather. Borne downhill by the flowing water, these pieces rub against the stream bed and wear it away. As the stream zig-zags fast downhill, it carves a narrow valley in the mountainside.

Tributaries

Other streams flow in to join it from both sides. These *tributaries* help the main stream to grow into a river. From the air it would look like a tree trunk, with all the tributary streams as branches. Each tributary carves its own valley. So what may have been a smooth hillside becomes a complicated maze of ridges with steep valleys in between.

Meanwhile, the bits of rock carried downstream by the river and its tributaries break into ever smaller pieces as they grind against the river bed and one another. In this way boulders become stones; stones form gravel; gravel turns to sand; and sand helps to make mud.

Lowland Rivers

When the river has left the mountains, it flows more gently through the land. It no longer deepens its bed, but flows in wide loops called *meanders*.

As the river works its way downstream it wears away the banks on either side and pushes them back. In time, the river flows lazily in huge meanders that wander across a low plain. At its mouth, the river's muddy water pours out to sea.

Water Underground

In limestone countryside, rocks are worn away invisibly beneath your feet by water flowing underground.

This is what happens. Falling rain collects a little carbon dioxide gas from the atmosphere. This turns rain into weak carbonic acid. Carbonic acid has the power to dissolve limestone.

Mountain limestone dissolves easily because it is seamed with tiny cracks that run across and up and down. What seems like solid rock is really just a mass of giant limestone 'bricks' packed very close together. Rainwater trickling into cracks in limestone widens the cracks by attacking their sides.

Clints, Grikes and Caves

In this way surface cracks become deep narrow fissures called *grikes*. The limestone blocks between grikes are known as *clints*.

In time, some cracks are widened into passages that lead underground. Streams vanish into swallowholes. They plunge down shafts then flow through caves they have carved in the mountain.

Fairy Palaces

Many limestone caves seem like fairy palaces. Smooth, gleaming *stalagmites* jut up from the floor. Spiky *stalactites* hang from the ceiling. A stalagmite and stalactite that meet produce a pillar. The world's tallest stands in a Spanish cave, and is almost 60 metres high.

Stalactites and stalagmites are built up of thin layers of calcite left behind as dripping water evaporates. The calcite comes from minerals dissolved from limestone.

Building a big stalagmite or stalactite may take up to thousands of years. But some grow as much as seven centimetres a year.

This diagram shows how water has attacked a limestone mountain.
(1) Clints and grikes
(2) Swallowholes (one now dry) widened by streams
(3) Caves (some now dry) carved by streams
(4) Stalagmites
(5) Stalactites
(6) Calcite pillar
(7) Stream outlet

Ice in Action

More than one-tenth of all the land on Earth lies under ice. Ice rivers called *glaciers* fill almost all the very high mountain valleys. Huge sheets of ice thick enough to swallow any skyscraper cover Antarctica and much of Greenland. Long ago, ice sheets also covered much of North America and Europe.

In all these places, moving ice has greatly changed the surface of the land.

Rocks Rasped by Ice
Valley glaciers are born where snow fills hollows high on mountainsides. Tightly packed snow turns to ice. If this spills from its hollow and creeps downhill a baby glacier is born. As it grows, a glacier will fill a valley carved out by a river in warmer times.

Many glaciers flow less than a metre a day. Yet they powerfully scour a valley floor and sides. This is because loose stones stuck in the moving ice rasp off bits of solid rock. When a glacier melts it leaves a broad, steep-sided valley.

Ice even alters mountain peaks. Ice hollows high up on a mountain 'eat' back toward

Snowfields high up in these mountains feed a small valley glacier.

the crest until they gnaw it into a sharp-edged ridge, or a pointed peak.

But if an ice sheet covers the whole mountain, it may grind it down to a low stub.

Nature's Rubbish Heaps
Rocks picked up by a moving glacier or ice sheet fall out when they reach its melting front or 'snout'.

Piles of rubble called *moraines* show where ice has melted in the European Alps and over parts of northern Germany. Streams flowing from glaciers and ice sheets have spread gravels, sands and clays far and wide.

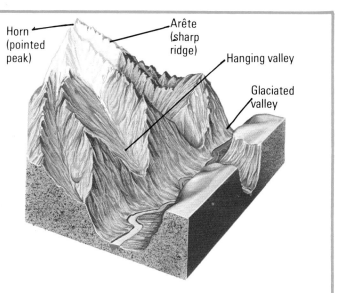

Horn (pointed peak)

Arête (sharp ridge)

Hanging valley

Glaciated valley

Above: Ice scooped out this glaciated valley and shortened ridges and valleys that ran in from the sides. This created hanging valleys above the main one. Frost and ice sharpened peaks and ridges.

Below: Two kinds of debris dumped by glaciers. *Drumlins* are sandy oval humps shaped by moving ice. *Eskers* are winding ridges of sand and gravel laid down by streams flowing from a glacier.

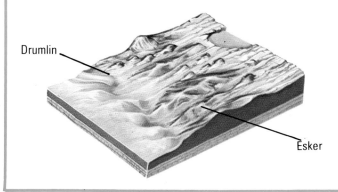

Drumlin

Esker

Desert Winds

A third of the world's land is desert. Here the ground is too dry to gain a covering of plants, and bare rock and loose stones lie open to attack by the wind. It is mainly the wind which shapes the surfaces of such deserts.

Sand-Blasted Rocks

Winds lack the force of glaciers or mountain rivers. They cannot shift big stones, but they can pick up smaller particles broken from the solid rock by weather. Winds send gravel hopping low across the ground. They blow the sand waist high. And they can send vast clouds of dust towering high up into the atmosphere.

Windblown sand does most to shape the deserts. Whirled along by wind, sands rasp with stinging force against the

Left: Windblown sand has scoured the base of this rock so it stands like a mushroom on a stalk.

Two dune types: A *barchan* (below) has ends curved by the wind blowing from left to right. A *seif* dune (right) is a long dune ridge, perhaps made of joined-up barchans.

rocks standing in their path. The sand carves grooves in soft rock. It gnaws caves low down in cliffs and rubs away the bases of boulders until they topple over.

Windblown sand has scooped huge 'saucers' in Africa's Sahara Desert—the largest desert of all. The Qattara Depression in Egypt is an immense hollow which lies below the level of the sea. It is almost as big as the area of Wales.

Seas of Sand

Sands scoured from one part of a desert may pile up somewhere else. The immense Sahara Desert includes huge seas of sand. Where the wind direction keeps shifting, the sands lie in smooth sheets. But where the wind blows steadily from one direction, sands pile up in hillocks called *dunes*. A dune will start to grow where a stone or bush slows down the flow of sand across the ground. As the dune grows, sands may blow across its top and down the other side. In time this shifts the whole dune forward. Some deserts contain row upon row of dunes, shifting so slowly that they look like frozen waves.

Desert winds also dump thick layers of fertile dust called *loess*. Loess blown from the Gobi Desert covers much of northwest China. Windblown dust made from rocks ground up by ancient ice sheets covers much of North America and parts of northern Europe.

Shifting Shores

Nowhere is the land more changeable than on the shorelines of the world. Some coasts are being swiftly washed away by waves, while others are growing out into the sea.

Waves carve caves in each side of a headland.

The caves meet, making an arch and a blowhole.

Retreating Cliffs

Sea cliffs show where sea attacks the land. As storm waves smash against the bottom of a cliff they force air into narrow cracks in the rock. The squashed air presses hard against the sides of the cracks. In time, air pressure widens the cracks and loosens the blocks of rock that stand between them.

When the rocks drop into the sea, waves hurl them hard against the bottom of the cliff. This breaks off more rock. In this way the sea wears away the cliff foot until the cliff top falls. Bit by bit, the cliff face retreats before the waves. In time, only a low rock platform seen at low tide shows where a cliff top used to stand.

Soft rock tends to wear away faster than hard rock. So bays form where soft rocks

The arch roof falls, leaving a rocky islet.

stood. Between such bays hard rock may remain jutting out as headlands.

Advancing Mudflats

Broken bits of rock removed from rocky shores are washed along the coast until they reach an obstacle. There they pile up on the shore as sloping beaches.

Storms sometimes sweep away such sand or shingle beaches. But mud lasts longer. Big rivers pour huge loads of mud into the sea. In shallow, sheltered river mouths, mud can pile up to form low islands called mudflats. Land plants help to bind the mud. In time the mud may build a *delta*—an apron of low land jutting out into the sea.

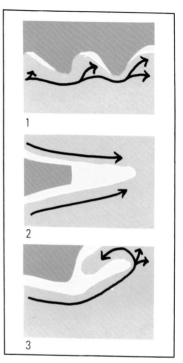

Above: How three kinds of beach are formed:
(1) Sand washed along a coast by currents and waves collects in bays as headlands block its path.
(2) Sand washed along both sides of a peninsula builds a beach beyond it.
(3) Sand washed along a coast builds a spit that juts out from a headland.

Left: A bar of sand and shingle has grown across a bay and trapped a shallow-water lagoon.

33

The Oceans

The salty waters of the oceans and seas cover most of the Earth's surface. Seas and oceans hold over thirty times more water than rivers, lakes, glaciers, ice sheets, soil, surface rocks and air combined.

The Mighty Oceans

By far the largest areas of seawater are the oceans. There are four of these huge, connected tracts of water.

The Pacific Ocean is easily the largest and deepest ocean. The Pacific lies east of Australia and Asia and west of the Americas, and stretches from the Arctic south through the tropics and into cold Antarctic regions. It is long and wide enough to swallow all the continents, and its deepest trench is more than deep enough to swallow Mount Everest, the world's highest mountain.

The Atlantic Ocean is the second largest ocean, but is less than half as large as the Pacific. The Atlantic lies east of the

Right: Oceans hold 97 per cent of all water.
Below: Water covers 71 per cent of the Earth.

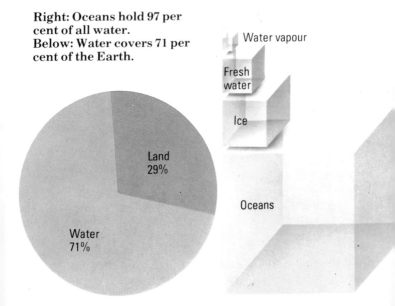

Water vapour

Fresh water

Ice

Land 29%

Oceans

Water 71%

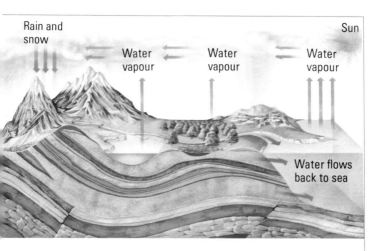

The Sun's heat sucks up water vapour from the sea and land. Cooled vapour turns to rain or snow. Rain that falls on the land flows in rivers back to the sea. This process forms the Earth's water cycle.

Americas and west of Europe and Africa. Like the Pacific Ocean, the Atlantic sprawls from the Arctic almost half way around the world.

The Indian Ocean is the third largest ocean. This ocean is nearly as large as the Atlantic and most of it is deeper than the Atlantic. The Indian Ocean lies between Africa, Asia, Australia and Antarctica.

The Arctic Ocean is the smallest and shallowest ocean. You could fit 13 oceans the size of it into the Pacific and leave room to spare. The Arctic Ocean is almost hemmed in by northern North America and northern Asia.

Seas Around the World

Seas are smaller than oceans. Most seas belong to oceans but are partly cut off from them by land. The largest sea is the South China Sea, which is part of the Pacific Ocean. Some large salt-water lakes are known as seas. The biggest of these inland seas is the Caspian Sea. It is almost as large as the nation of Japan.

Surprising Seawater

There is more to seawater than just a salty taste. Scientists have learnt some surprising facts about the substances the sea contains; about the temperature of the sea in different places; and about its pressure at different depths.

Chemicals in Seawater

About 35 parts in every 1000 parts of seawater are not water at all but other substances. About 29 of these 35 parts are actually common salt. But seawater also holds many scarcer chemicals like magnesium sulphate, calcium, and potassium bicarbonate. There are even tiny quantities of gold.

Some chemicals found in seawater dissolved from the seabed. Others have been washed into the sea by rivers. Seawater can evaporate but its chemicals cannot. Yet more are being added all the time. So the sea is saltier than it was when oceans began millions of years ago.

Some seas are saltier than others. The Red Sea is in a hot climate and evaporation is high. It has 38 parts of salts per 1000. But the Baltic Sea is in a cool climate and is fed with fresh water by rivers, so areas of this sea have only two parts of salts per 1000.

Hot and Cold

The surface temperature of a sea depends largely on how near it is to the equator. Shallow, narrow waters in the tropics can reach 36°C— the temperature of the Persian Gulf in summer. But areas of polar ocean are always frozen. Deep down, oceans everywhere are cold. If you took ocean temperatures at all depths the average would be a chilly 4°C.

Ocean Pressure

At sea level, water pressure acts on objects with about the same force as the air just above. But water pressure increases with depth. In the lowest depths of the Pacific Ocean water pressure is over 1100 times as great as sea-level air pressure—enough to crush an ordinary submarine to pulp.

Devices lowered from a ship can tell us much about the waters of the deepest oceans and the ocean floor beneath.

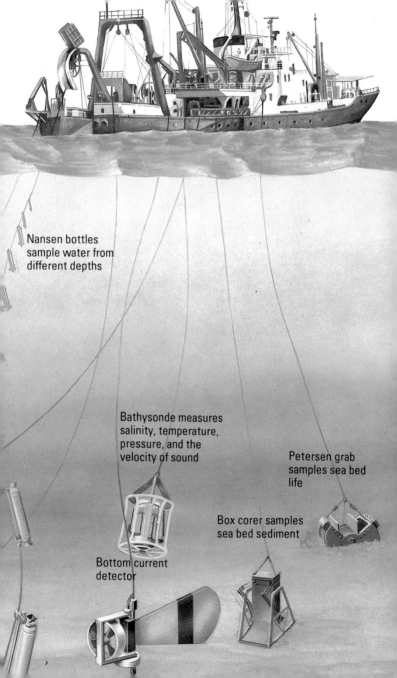

Nansen bottles sample water from different depths

Bathysonde measures salinity, temperature, pressure, and the velocity of sound

Petersen grab samples sea bed life

Box corer samples sea bed sediment

Bottom current detector

Waves and Tides

Waves and tides help to keep the seas in continual motion. Waves are set in motion by the wind. Tides are caused by the Earth's spin and the pulls exerted by the Moon and Sun.

Waves at Work

Waves look like ridges of moving water. But out at sea water does not travel with the waves. The waves pass through water in the same way that ripples pass through a rope if you shake it from one end. So passing waves simply make floating objects bob up and down in one place.

This is what happens. Each wave crest shifts water particles back, up, forward, down and then back again. So the surface water travels in a circle. But this starts water circling lower down. Below each wave crest is a whole stack of circling water particles (see diagram).

If the lowest circling particles drag on the sea bed the whole stack of particles above slows down. Wave crests catch up with one another, rear up and topple over. Waves begin to break onto the shore as they reach shallower water less than half a wave-length deep. (A wave-length is the distance between two wave crests.)

Storm Waves

The faster the wind blows the higher and longer waves become. Strong winds can build long, smooth waves called swells. Some measure one kilometre from one wave crest to the next. Storms have created waves as high as 34 metres.

Tsunami—waves set off by undersea earthquakes—can be twice as high as that.

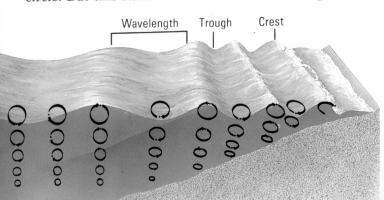

Wavelength   Trough   Crest

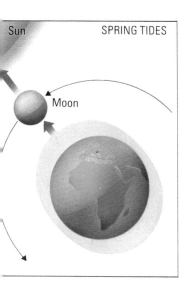

Sun SPRING TIDES

Moon

**Above: Spring tide—Sun and Moon pull together.
Below: Neap tide—they pull in different directions.**

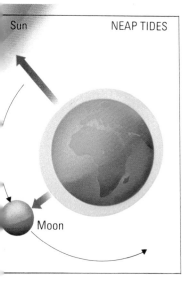

Sun NEAP TIDES

Moon

A tsunami may travel almost as fast as a jet airliner. Out at sea the wave is barely high enough to be seen. But some sweep far inland and drown whole villages.

How Tides Happen

Once a day two tides travel round the world, rather like two huge, slow-moving waves. High tides are caused by the ocean water piling up until its surface bulges above the normal sea level. One bulge is caused by the pulling force exerted by the Moon upon the Earth. The other bulge happens on the far side of the Earth, as the Earth's spin tries to throw ocean water outward into space.

Low tides are the troughs left by the water that has been pulled away by the high-tide bulges.

The Sun affects tides too. When Sun and Moon line up and pull together we get spring tides—high high tides and low low tides. When Sun and Moon pull at right angles we get neap tides—low high tides and high low tides. Spring tides and neap tides both occur twice a month.

Some bays have tides high enough to drown a house. But almost landlocked seas like the Mediterranean have hardly any tides at all.

Ocean Currents

Much as rivers flow across the land, belts of water flow through the oceans. Some of these ocean currents are huge. The West Wind Drift carries over 2000 times more water than the Amazon—the largest river in the world.

How Ocean Currents Flow

Winds start currents moving. But currents must change course to go around continents. Then, too, the Earth's spin makes currents veer right in the northern hemisphere and veer left in the southern hemisphere. All this helps to keep surface currents circling the oceans. Warm surface currents from the tropics carry heat toward the cold polar regions.

OCEAN CURRENTS

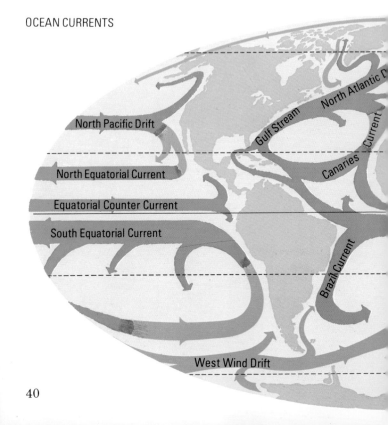

North Pacific Drift

North Equatorial Current

Equatorial Counter Current

South Equatorial Current

Gulf Stream

North Atlantic D

Canaries

Current

Brazil Current

West Wind Drift

Meanwhile cold water from the polar regions sinks below this warmer water and flows toward the tropics. In parts of the tropics, cold water wells up from deep down to take the place of water carried off by surface currents. Water rising from deep down is rich in minerals that help to nourish ocean plants and animals.

Ocean Currents and Climate

Warm and cold ocean currents heat or cool the air above them. In this way, currents warm or cool nearby coasts. For instance the cold Labrador Current helps to give eastern Canada cold winters. But the warm North Atlantic Drift keeps western Scotland's winters mild. Eastern Canada and western Scotland lie equally far north—but different currents give them different climates.

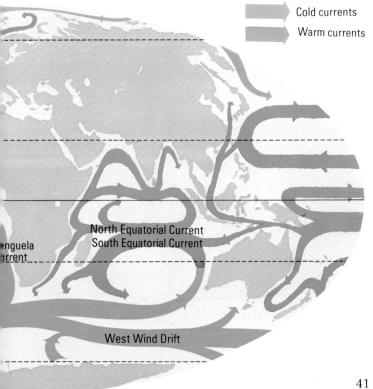

Cold currents
Warm currents

North Equatorial Current
South Equatorial Current
nguela
rrent
West Wind Drift

Underwater Landscape

Imagine skimming just above the sea bed in a deep-sea submarine travelling from Europe to Central America.

First you would cross a *continental shelf*. This is an underwater plateau which is never any deeper than 180 metres. Old cliffs and river beds show that parts of it were once above the sea. Here and there rivers and currents have heaped up banks of gravel, sand and mud. Continental shelves—some broad, some narrow—fringe all the continents.

An Underwater Wall
Beyond the continental shelf, the sea floor slants downward for about 3800 metres. This tremendous *continental slope* is sometimes called the world's mightiest boundary wall. Deep gashes pierce the wall where the strong ocean currents have torn out gravel, sand and mud.

Peaks and Trenches
Below the continental slope stretch the vast plains of the deep-sea region known as the *abyss*.

Beyond these plains rises a mighty chain of underwater mountains built by molten rock welling from a crack that runs north-south through the middle of the Atlantic Ocean floor.

You cross another deep-sea plain, before, off the West Indies, plunging into a deep, narrow trench where the ocean floor is disappearing down into the mantle. Next come islands, then another continental shelf, and mainland Central America.

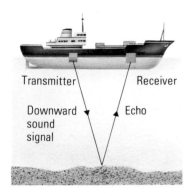

Transmitter   Receiver

Downward sound signal   Echo

Left: Echo-sounders measure depth as the time taken for a sound to reach the sea bed and echo back.

Right: Some of the main features of the ocean floor. More than 97 per cent of ocean water lies below the continental shelf. Only special craft can plumb these depths.

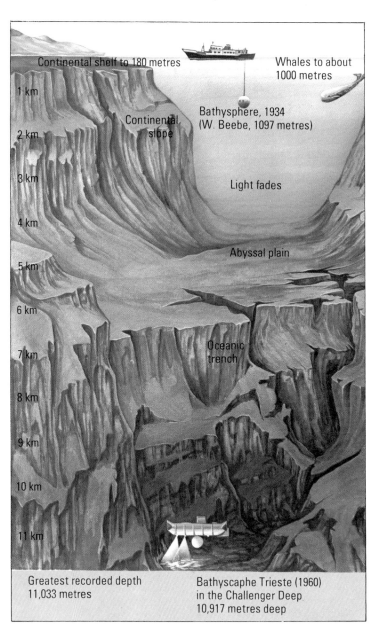

Continental shelf to 180 metres

Whales to about 1000 metres

1 km

2 km

3 km

4 km

5 km

6 km

7 km

8 km

9 km

10 km

11 km

Continental slope

Bathysphere, 1934
(W. Beebe, 1097 metres)

Light fades

Abyssal plain

Oceanic trench

Greatest recorded depth
11,033 metres

Bathyscaphe Trieste (1960)
in the Challenger Deep
10,917 metres deep

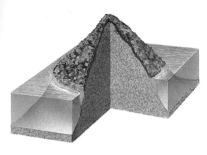

This volcanic island is rimmed by a stony reef built by coral polyps—tiny creatures of warm, clear, shallow waters.

The volcano is sinking but the coral keeps on growing upward. So the reef can still be seen.

The volcanic island has sunk, leaving the reef as a low circular coral island called an *atoll*.

Islands

Here and there, islands jut above the surfaces of oceans and seas. Some are small enough for waves to splash their tops. Others are immense. Greenland, the largest island, is almost four times as big as France.

Oceanic Islands

One day in 1963 a ship was sailing in the chilly northern Atlantic Ocean when it reached a patch of boiling water. Days later the sea opened and the smoking top of a volcano thrust above the waves. In three weeks it had built a brand new island almost one kilometre across. People in nearby Iceland named it Surtsey, after an old fire god.

Surtsey is one of thousands of oceanic islands, so named because they sprout steeply from the mid-ocean floor.

Much farther south in the Atlantic lie other oceanic islands, such as St Paul's Rocks and Ascension Island. All were built by volcanic rock, rising from the crack running down the middle of the vast underwater Mid-Atlantic Ridge.

Thousands more oceanic islands stand in the Pacific

Ocean. Many others now lie beneath the surface. Some had their tops worn down by waves. Others drowned when the ocean floor below tilted and began to slide down into the Earth's mantle.

Island Arcs

Japan, Sumatra and Java, and New Zealand belong to curving rows of islands known as island arcs. Such islands grow where two of the plates making up the Earth's crust collide and one is pushed below the other. These islands are partly fold mountains thrust up by the colliding plates. But they include volcanoes fed by molten rock that has escaped up through the crust.

The Florida Keys are low islands. Many are just loose sand piled up by the sea in shallow water, often on a bed of coral.

Continental Islands

Islands made of rocks that once belonged to nearby continents are called continental islands. Great Britain, Ireland and Newfoundland are three examples. When the sea level was lower than it is today, stretches of land joined Ireland and Great Britain to the rest of Europe.

The islands Borneo, Java and Sumatra were once part of a huge south-east Asian peninsula. Geographers have named that vanished region Sundaland.

The Air Around Us

We live at the bottom of an invisible ocean—the mixed gases that form the Earth's atmosphere. Other planets have atmospheres, but only ours is mainly made of nitrogen and oxygen—ingredients all living things depend on. Air also includes tiny amounts of other gases. It holds particles of dust and water vapour, too.

The Layered Atmosphere
There are five layers in our atmosphere. First comes the *troposphere*. This is only 8 to 16 kilometres thick, but it has most of the air. Here, living things breathe, clouds form, winds blow and rain and snow fall. Temperature drops as you rise through the troposphere.

The second atmospheric layer is the *stratosphere*. This contains ozone, a type of oxygen that helps to shut out harmful radiation from the Sun.

About 50 kilometres up, the stratosphere gives way to the *mesosphere*—the coldest region in the atmosphere.

The *ionosphere* begins some 80 kilometres up. This layer is more than 400 kilometres thick. Rays from space bombard and ionize (electrically charge) its particles.

Above the ionosphere come the thinly scattered gases of the *exosphere*, which stretches far out into space.

Left: Air is a thin skin of gases clinging to the Earth's surface.

Right: Weather happens in the troposphere. In or above the stratosphere, meteors burn up, cosmic rays hit atoms in the air, noctilucent dust clouds form. In the ionosphere, solar particles produce coloured lights called auroras.

46

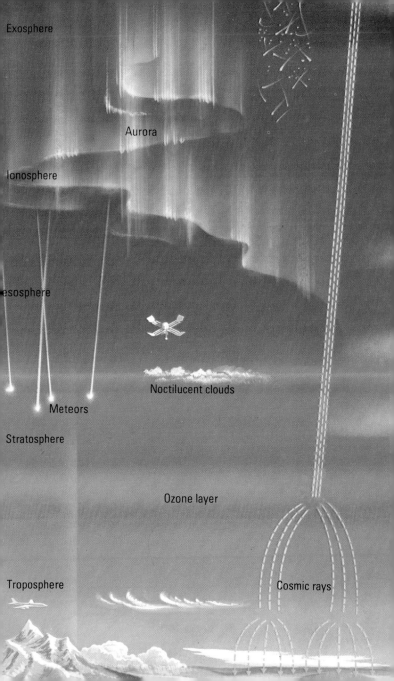

Exosphere

Aurora

Ionosphere

esosphere

Noctilucent clouds

Meteors

Stratosphere

Ozone layer

Troposphere

Cosmic rays

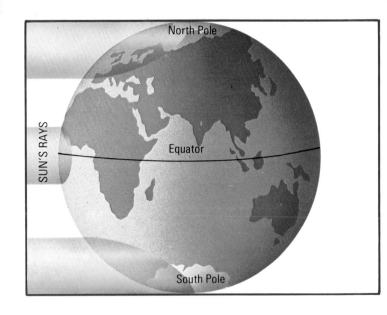

Labels: North Pole, SUN'S RAYS, Equator, South Pole

Sun and Wind

Only a tiny fraction of the Sun's energy is beamed down to the Earth. But we receive enough to keep our planet's surface warm. Air does much to trap the Sun's heat, and moving air spreads that heat around the world.

Lost Sunshine
Less than half of the Sun's energy beamed at the Earth actually reaches the surface of the sea and the land. About one-fifth is trapped by the Earth's atmosphere.

Nearly one-third of the incoming energy is bounced back into space off clouds and dust in the atmosphere. Some of the Sun's rays bounce off particles of water vapour, dust and air molecules. Blue light is scattered most. This is why the sky seems blue when we look up on a sunny day.

Nature's Greenhouse
Some of the energy that reaches land or water also bounces back up. This leaves only about one-third of all incoming energy to heat the continents and oceans.

As these warm up, they give off heat that helps to

warm the air above them. In fact the atmosphere traps nearly three-quarters of the heat escaping from the Earth.

Air acts like a greenhouse roof—it lets in the short-wave energy arriving from the Sun but traps long-wave heat energy escaping from the Earth.

In this way air helps to stop temperatures falling very low at night and in winter—times when the Earth's surface loses more energy than it receives.

The World's Winds

Sunshine heats some places more than others. But moving air spreads the heat around.

Air moving to and fro over the world creates the winds.

Hot, light air rises in the doldrums and flows north and south. In the horse latitudes it cools, grows heavy and sinks. Some flows back toward the equator. Some flows toward the poles and meets cold air flowing toward the equator. The Earth's spin affects the direction of the wind.

Below: Trade winds are warm winds. Westerlies are mixed warm and cold air. Polar easterlies are cold polar winds.

MAJOR WIND BELTS

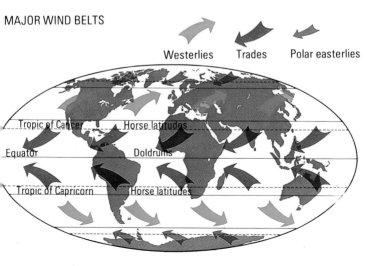

Westerlies   Trades   Polar easterlies

Tropic of Cancer   Horse latitudes

Equator   Doldrums

Tropic of Capricorn   Horse latitudes

Climate

Climate is the expected pattern of weather year by year. The amount of sunshine, rain, snow, frost and wind all go to make up climate.

Hot and Cold

The hottest climates are in the tropics—regions close to the equator. Here the Sun shines directly overhead at midday on at least one day each year.

The polar regions of the far north and far south have the coldest climates. North of the Arctic Circle and south of the Antarctic Circle the Sun does not rise at all on at least one day each year.

Between the tropics and polar regions lie regions with temperate climates. These places tend to have warm summers and cool winters.

But the temperature does not drop evenly as you go from

Above: Flimsy rainproof huts set in the polar climate of the Arctic north. Here, winter lasts for nine months.

Below: Flimsy rainproof huts are shelter enough in the warm, moist climate of the tropical rain forests.

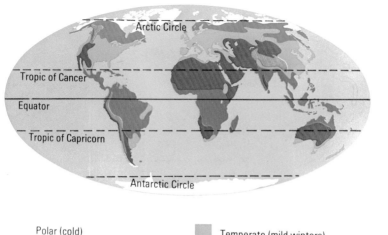

Polar (cold)

Mountain (cold, windy)

Cold forest (cold winters)

Temperate (mild winters)

Desert (dry)

Tropical rainy (warm, moist)

the equator to the poles. This is partly because continents warm up and cool down more readily than oceans. Also, mountain ranges and coasts can block or turn aside winds and ocean currents. So warm tropical air and water and cold polar air and water travel farther across the world in some places than they do in others (see page 41).

Then, too, the higher you climb the colder it gets. High mountain tops—even in the tropics—are always cold.

Wet and Dry

Like heat, rain is spread unevenly around the world. Rain falls where moist air cools and its water vapour turns to water drops too heavy to remain in the air.

In moist tropical regions the Sun sucks up a lot of water vapour. This cools as it rises until it changes into raindrops. In temperate regions, much of the rain falls where warm, moist sub-tropical air is forced up and covers cold air from the polar regions.

Air which has passed over the sea is moister than inland air, so places near the oceans are usually rainier than places far inland.

Weather

Weather is the state of the air hour by hour or day by day. Places near the equator have much the same weather all year round. For instance, in Malaysia you can always expect a bright, sunny morning; a cloudy, rainy afternoon; and a temperature close to 27°C.

Temperate regions have more varied weather. In the British Isles, a cool rainy morning may give way to a warm, sunny afternoon, followed by a frosty night with gales and rain next day.

Depressions

Temperate regions have such varied weather because they are often crossed by *depressions*. These are like giant eddies in the *polar front*— the boundary between warm sub-tropical air blowing toward the polar regions, and cold polar air blowing toward the tropics.

Each 'eddy' or depression is a whirling mass of warm and cold low-pressure air, 300 to 1500 kilometres across.

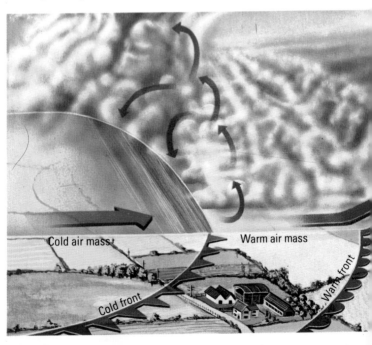

Cold air mass
Warm air mass
Cold front
Warm front

In the northern hemisphere, winds blow anticlockwise round a depression. In the southern hemisphere, the winds blow clockwise.

Inside a depression, warm moist air overtakes and rises above cold air. More cold air catches up the warm air from behind and undercuts it.

As the warm air rises it cools and water vapour forms droplets that build clouds. Inside the clouds these droplets merge to make big, heavy drops that fall as rain.

Depressions, then, bring rainy, windy weather.

Anticyclones

Temperate regions sometimes have days of settled sunny weather. This is due to *anticyclones* — high-pressure air systems. In an anticyclone, winds blow in the opposite direction to those in a depression.

A depression moving from left to right. Wedged between cold air masses, warm air rises, cools and sheds rain. Drizzle falls ahead of the warm front. Showers fall behind the cold front.

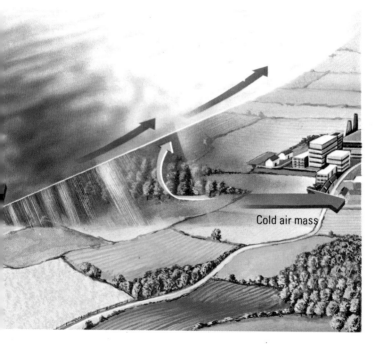

Cold air mass

Life on Earth

Life began more than 3500 million years ago. Some of the earliest living things were tiny plant-like organisms in the sea. True plants, and also animals, came later. At first none lived on land.

Life Gets Complicated

Tiny, simple sea creatures developed into larger, more complicated kinds. By 600 million years ago, sea worms were burrowing into the sea bed. Trilobites—looking like big, broad woodlice—crawled around on jointed legs. From animals with jointed legs came millipedes and scorpions. Such creepy-crawlies were among the first animals to move onto the land.

By 500 million years ago, wormlike animals were giving rise to fishes—the first animals with a back-bone to support the body from inside. Certain fishes developed lungs and

Fossils of long-dead animals and plants:
(1) Mould (left) and cast of a trilobite.
(2) Petrified log—wood replaced by minerals.
(3) Carbon smear of a prehistoric fern.
(4) Fossil teeth from prehistoric beasts.
(5) Footprints in mud, now turned to stone.

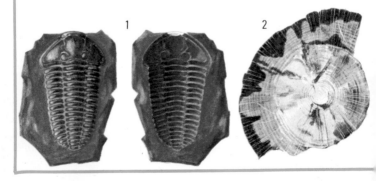

sturdy fins and spent some time on land. From them came frogs and other amphibians, which can live on land but must lay eggs in water.

Amphibians led to reptiles like snakes and lizards. By 150 million years ago early reptiles had given rise to mammals and birds.

Records in Rocks

All the main groups of animals we have mentioned live today, but in each group there are many kinds that have died out. We know what some of these were like from their fossils.

When something dies its shape may be preserved in rock. These preserved shapes are called fossils. A fossil may form if a dead animal or plant sinks to a muddy sea bed. Mud piling up around it protects its hard parts from decay. These parts slowly dissolve, but are replaced by minerals which change them into stone. Meanwhile, the surrounding mud is buried under more layers of mud and turns to rock. If the rock gets pushed above the sea, weather may wear it away and the fossils appear on the surface.

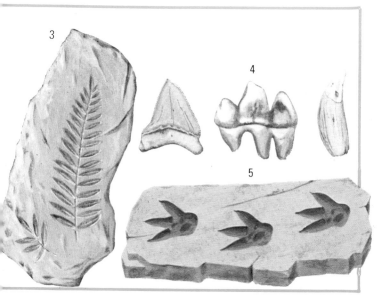

The Living Soil

Asked to name the most valuable substance found on land some people might say, 'Diamonds'. A much better answer would be, 'Soil'.

Soil forms only a thin surface layer above the rocks that make up the Earth's crust. But without soil most land plants would not grow, and without plants animals would starve. Most of the crops and animals that we feed on would disappear.

What Soil Does
Soil helps plants in several important ways.

First, it provides them with a roothold. Rain and wind cannot wash or blow away plants that are firmly rooted in the soil.

Next, soil holds the moisture and foods that plants suck up through their roots.

Thirdly, soil stores heat and this helps plants to grow, especially in spring and autumn when the air loses much of its warmth at night.

Types of Soil
Well developed soil has three main layers. Usually the top

Rain washes all but a thin surface layer of plant food deep down in this podzol soil.

layer is rich in dark humus —the broken down remains of plants and animals.

The second layer may be humus mixed with sand and tiny stones. The third layer is mainly of stones that weather has broken from the solid rock beneath.

Different soils have particles of different sizes. There are light sandy soils with large particles and large gaps between them. Clay soils have small particles and small gaps. Loamy soils have particles of mixed sizes, and are very rich in humus.

This grassland soil has less rain than podzol soil. Plant food stays near the surface.

Water evaporating from this hot desert soil leaves a salty crust where few plants grow.

Soil type depends partly on the rocks beneath the ground, but largely on the climate of the region.

Soils and Climates

The tundra soils of the far north have a peaty layer on top. Then comes bluish mud. Below that is a layer of sub-soil that is frozen all the year.

Podzols form in cool, rainy climates. Many have a grey upper layer with little humus. Lower down are thin, hard layers of humus and other substances.

Huge dryish regions of North America and Russia have rich, dark soils called black earths or chernozems.

Rainy tropical climates produce brick-red soils called laterites. Their name comes from the Latin word for 'brick'. Heavy rains tend to wash their goodness deep down.

Hot deserts have reddish brown soils with salts sucked up by hot sunshine.

The brown forest soils of western Europe are rich in humus made from the rotted leaves of oak, ash and other forest trees.

Above: Cactuses hold in moisture. These plants can thrive in deserts.
Below: Banana plants lose moisture easily. They need a warm, damp climate.

Where Plants Live

Geographers divide the world into natural regions, each with its special set of plants. You would pass through at least seven natural regions if you journeyed south from the Arctic through Eastern Europe and Africa to the equator.

Plants of the North
In the tundra region of the cold far north only lichens, mosses, flowers, small shrubs and dwarf trees grow. Frost and cold winds would kill most other kinds of plant.

South of the tundra lies the taiga. This is a huge belt of

Right: A climb up a tall peak at the equator takes you through the same plant zones that stretch at sea level from the equator to the far north.

Ice and snow   Mosses and lichen

58

forest made up of conifers—needle-leaved trees that bear their seeds in cones. Conifers are able to survive long, cold winters.

Farther south again are the deciduous forests. Here grow oaks, beeches and other broad-leaved trees that shed their leaves in winter.

In the dry lands of eastern Europe the short grasses of the steppes take the place of forest trees.

Plants of Warm Lands

The lands that fringe the Mediterranean Sea have long, hot, dry summers. Here the trees and shrubs have tough leaves to retain water.

To the south sprawls the Sahara Desert where it is always hot and dry. Some desert plants have thorny leaves, which hold moisture and keep away animals that feed on leaves.

South of the Sahara are the tall tropical grasses and scattered trees of the savanna.

At the equator the tropical rain forests grow. Tall broad-leaved trees meet high above the dim, dark forest floor.

Mountain Plants

The temperature falls as you rise above sea level. High in the mountains the climate may be as cold as the tundra, even though a mountain is at the equator. Plants that grow on high mountains are similar to those in the Arctic, regardless of where the mountain is.

undra   Coniferous forest   Deciduous forest   Tropical forest

Animal Regions

For millions of years oceans, mountains or deserts have cut off some groups of creatures from others. Isolated groups have developed differently from the rest. Zoologists divide the world today into six animal regions, each with its own set of wild animals.

Northern Regions

Northern lands have two animal regions. Only the *Nearctic Region* of North America has the antelope-like pronghorn, the bowfin (a freshwater fish) and certain families of lizards. Hedge sparrows are found only in the *Palaearctic Region*, which mostly lies in Europe. But Nearctic and Palaearctic share beavers, grouse, perches and salamanders. In fact zoologists often lump both regions together and call them the *Holarctic Region*.

Animal regions of the world. The pronghorn, hippopotamus and kangaroo each live in a separate region with no close kin elsewhere. But the horse and the Indian elephant are related to the zebra and the African elephant of the Ethiopian Region.

Nearctic Region

(Pronghorn antelope)

Neotropical Region

(Giant anteater)

Southern Regions

The *Ethiopian Region* (mainly in Africa) is the home of the hippopotamus, hyrax, and ostrich. Africa shares many bird families with southern Asia, the *Oriental Region*. But this has its own creatures, like flying lemurs, tree shrews and fairy bluebirds. For a long time, South America (the *Neotropical Region*) was separate from any other land mass, and Australasia (the *Australian Region*) has been separate for even longer. This is partly why they have so many unusual beasts. All of South America's 'old-fashioned' mammals were killed off when more 'modern' kinds moved in from North America. But only the Neotropical Region has true anteaters, New World monkeys, and sloths.

Australasia contains the strangest animals of all. Its platypus and echidna are the only mammals that lay eggs. Here, too, live the kangaroos, koalas, wombats and most other marsupials—mammals whose females bear tiny undeveloped young and tend to rear them in a belly pouch.

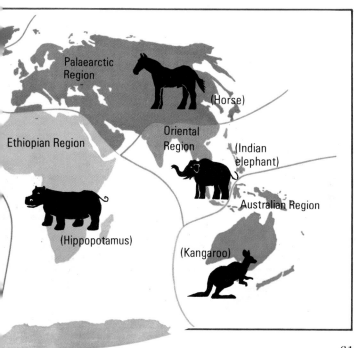

Palaearctic Region

(Horse)

Oriental Region

Ethiopian Region

(Indian elephant)

Australian Region

(Hippopotamus)

(Kangaroo)

The Human World

Man is probably the world's most plentiful and widespread mammal. There are more than 4000 million people living on the Earth today.

People come in a surprising variety of sizes, shapes and colours. These differences originally came about in people who lived in different climates. Thus brown skins helped protect Africans and other dark-skinned people from the harmful rays of hot sunshine in the tropics. Pale skins helped Caucasian (white) people to benefit from the weak sunshine of cloudy northern Europe. Short arms and legs helped the ancestors of the Chinese to survive cold regions of northern Asia.

Today, most dark-skinned people still live in the tropics, and most pale-skinned people live in cooler climates. But people of all kinds and colours have spread around the world. Nowadays many Africans live in the Americas and Europe.

Above: Chinese people belong to a racial group known as Mongoloid.

Left: Mestizos are of mixed Caucasian and Amerindian stock.

Above: Sri Lankans are dark-skinned Caucasians, related to Europeans.

Most of the people who live in North and South America, Australia and New Zealand are descended from European settlers. Chinese and Indian people have also made their homes in many lands. There are also many people in the world who have descended from families of mixed nationality and colour.

Language, Religion and Nationality

Difference in skin colour is one of the least of the differences that now separate people from one another.

Mankind has invented nearly 3000 languages. Most of us speak only one and cannot understand the rest. People have also developed different faiths. There are 11 main religions in the world today. Then, too, different groups of people have formed different nations. By the early 1980s there were more than 160 nations, some huge, some tiny.

Differences in race, language, faith and nationality help to divide peoples—but not everywhere. In many countries a mixture of people of different races, languages, faiths and nationalities live peacefully together.

Wealth from Soil and Water

About 8000 years ago, people in some parts of the world began growing crops and keeping animals for food. Stone Age farmers and herdsmen had found a surer supply of food than Stone Age hunters and foragers. So farming spread around the world and, as fewer people starved to death, the human population began to grow.

With no need to forage for food, farmers settled down in villages. They produced more food than they needed for themselves. Other people became full-time craftsmen and traded with the farmers.

So farming villages grew into towns and even cities. Few of us now produce the food we eat, but we all still depend on farmers for food.

The Plants We Prize

Farming is still the most important industry on Earth. About one-tenth of all land is ploughed or dug for growing crops. This is called *arable* farming.

Nearly two-thirds of all arable land grows cereals: grains like barley, wheat, maize and rice.

Other important food crops are fruits, vegetables and oil-producing plants. Crops that are not foods include cotton, rubber and cocoa. Forage crops like grass feed farm animals.

Most food crops that we eat come from temperate climates. But other useful crops grow in the tropics.

Both cool and warm forests provide timber. The northern conifers yield softwood and pulp for making paper. Hardwood trees from farther south are used for making furniture.

Living Larders

One-fifth of all land is used as *pasture* for farming livestock such as cows, goats, horses, sheep and poultry. Farm animals provide meat, eggs and milk, as well as wool, and skins for clothes.

Like Stone Age people we still hunt for fish. But modern fishing fleets bring in huge catches from the cool, fish-rich seas.

Right: Oxen plough rice fields in India. Rice grows in the moist, tropical regions.

Inset: Combine harvesters cut wheat on the cool grasslands of North America.

Riches From Rocks

Soil and water nourish the plants and animals we eat, but many of our tools, machines and buildings come from rocks below the soil.

Some rocks are particularly rich in minerals. The most valuable minerals include the so-called ores. Ores are minerals that contain enough of a metal to make mining it worthwhile. Iron, copper, lead, tin and zinc are among the many metals that we get from ores. Uranium ore is valuable as a source of atomic power.

But useful mineral deposits are scattered unevenly around the world. Finding them requires special tools and skills. Geologists map the surface rocks. Instruments called magnetometers help them to discover iron, and Geiger counters can show up the radioactive substance uranium. Gravimeters and seismographs help to build up a picture of the rock layers deep underground.

Right: Shiny cars are made in factories. But their ingredients are dull lumps of rock dug up from underground.

Quarrying and Mining

Mineral deposits near the surface are easily removed. Workers quarry gravel, sand and stone. Iron and copper ores are scooped from open-cast mines by giant power shovels.

But miners may have to tunnel through solid rock to reach minerals that lie deep down. One gold mine goes down almost four kilometres into the ground.

Often, huge mounds and pits are left where we have burrowed for the riches of the rocks.

From Mine to Factory

Once ores are mined they must be treated to separate the metals from impurities. For instance iron ore is heated in a blast furnace. Intense heat melts the iron, which is then collected as a liquid that hardens as it cools.

Left: An open-cast iron-ore mine in Australia. Here, a hill holds so much iron that miners need not tunnel for it. Machines just cut out huge chunks of the hill.

Mixing pure metals with certain other substances produces alloys that may be extra strong or tough, or special in some other way.

Lastly, factory machines shape the metal into tools and engines. Cars, radios, cookers and many more such objects were made in factories from substances extracted from the rocks.

67

Fuel and Power

Early people had to rely on their muscles fuelled by the food they ate to provide energy for shifting loads.

We have machines and engines far more powerful than any human body. Such inventions can shift huge loads. Others can light and heat whole cities. Many engines get their energy from *fossil fuels.*

Fuel From Underground

Fossil fuels are fuels formed many millions of years ago, when the remains of certain living things were trapped beneath the ground.

Coal is the remains of pre-

historic trees that grew in swamps about 300 million years ago. Thick layers of dead trees were drowned by the sea, then crushed as layers of mud and sand piled up above them. This pressure helped to slowly change the timber into coal.

Oil and natural gas are the remains of tiny animals and plants that lived in ancient shallow seas. Movements of the Earth's crust trapped them underground in tiny spaces between the particles that make up certain types of rock.

Miners scoop coal from shallow pits, or tunnel underground and cut it from the solid rocks. Oil and gas rise through holes drilled deep into the Earth's crust. At least one gas well has been driven 9·5 kilometres deep.

Energy From Water

Some waterfalls and fast-flowing rivers are made to spin huge wheels called turbines. These generate electric current. So do turbines spun by steam from water heated by burning coal, gas or oil.

Left: Machines that bite through solid rock cut coal in mines that reach deep under the ground.

In fact these fuels and flowing water are the Sun's energy at second hand. Sunlight produced the plants that helped form coal, gas and oil. The Sun's heat sucks up water vapour that falls as rain and feeds the rivers.

Nuclear Energy

Uranium produces energy without the Sun's help. Particles collide with and split the nuclei (the centres) of the atoms that make up uranium. These collisions give off heat that is used to generate electric current.

Above right: Waste gas is burnt off above a desert gas field in Algeria.

Below: A diagram shows the world's increasing need for energy and the different fuels that we use to supply that energy.

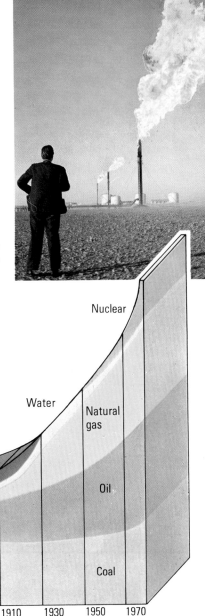

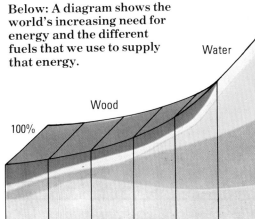

Nuclear

Water

Natural gas

Wood

Oil

100%

Coal

1830 1850 1870 1890 1910 1930 1950 1970

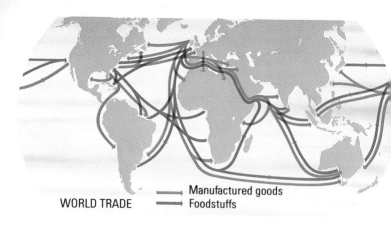

WORLD TRADE   → Manufactured goods
                  ⇒ Foodstuffs

Trade and Transport

Nations that produce more than they need of a product, sell the excess to other countries and buy the things they lack. In this way huge quantities of food, manufactured goods and raw materials like minerals travel around the world.

Buying and Selling Abroad
The goods that a nation sells abroad are known as *exports*. The goods that it buys from abroad are *imports*. Goods that you can see and handle are called visible imports and exports. But services like banking, insurance and tourism count as invisible imports and exports.

Some countries buy and sell far more than others. The major trading nations are the United States, West Germany and Japan. Such industrialized nations sell products manufactured by their many factories. They buy fuel and raw materials to keep those factories supplied. Britain is an industrialized nation that exports a third of what it makes and imports half its raw materials and food.

Developing countries have fewer factories than industrialized nations. So they import manufactured goods and pay for these by selling food and raw materials. Between them, developing countries like Colombia and Ghana supply much of the world's coffee and cocoa.

Left: This map shows that much of the world's trade flows to and from Europe and North America.

Right: Old-style donkey transport in modern Syria.

Below: Stowed in containers, goods go by sea and land.

How Goods Travel

Modern transport methods move vast amounts of goods by land, water and air. Industrialized nations have by far the world's best transport systems.

On land, heavy loads like coal or iron go by train. Vans and lorries transport many manufactured goods. Gas, petroleum and water are mostly carried through pipes.

Big tankers, ore carriers and container ships take huge loads across the oceans, and barges sail up rivers and canals. Water transport is slow but cheaper than all other kinds.

Passengers and costly goods often go by air. Flying is the fastest but the most expensive way to travel.

71

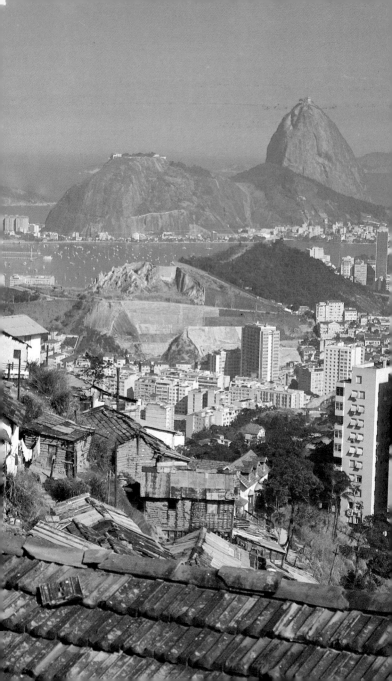

How People Live

Modern farming, mining and manufacturing machines have changed the way of life of people in industrialized nations.

New farming methods mean that three or four farm workers can produce enough to feed 100 people. So the other 96 or 97 need not work upon the land. Instead, most work in mines or factories, or in services like schools, hospitals, offices and shops.

These jobs bring people from the countryside into towns and cities. This helps to explain why cities have grown larger. By 1980, Tokyo and Mexico City each had about 10 million citizens and many major cities of the world were growing fast.

Haves and Have Nots

Some people are far better off than others. Developed countries produce goods and services that make life more

Shacks and skyscrapers show poverty and wealth side by side in Rio de Janeiro. Here, in Brazil, many poor people lack proper homes.

healthy, easy and pleasant for most of their citizens. Thus many European, North American, Japanese and Australasian families have homes, cars, television sets, and labour-saving machines such as dishwashers and vacuum cleaners.

Life is harsher in the world's poorer countries. Many South American, African and Asian nations cannot make or pay for the kinds of farm and factory machinery rich nations use.

Eight in every ten Chinese must work upon the land to grow enough to feed themselves and their families. Very few South Americans, Africans or Asians can afford the household aids that other people enjoy. If they fall ill, few ever see a doctor. Millions of people have too little food to eat and many die extremely young.

Multiplying Numbers

The human population is increasing fast each year. It has more than doubled since 1930. By AD 2020 it may have doubled yet again.

Population rises fastest in the poorest countries. But they already have too little food. How to feed the ever-increasing number of people is an enormous problem.

A Plundered Planet

The more people there are the more they need. People now use more food, water, timber, fuel and minerals than ever before. Getting these has greatly changed the surface of the Earth.

Destroying our Earth

To make room for such things as farms, mines, roads and cities, people have drained swamps, felled forests and even removed topsoil. Some of our activities have badly damaged land, water, air and living things.

Where swamp or forest is destroyed, the animals that live there die. Where careless farmers rob the soil of nourishment, plants die and soil is blown or washed away.

Factories and cars pour poisonous gases into the air. Pesticides, sewage and wastes from factories and ships pour into rivers, lakes and seas, where they kill water plants and animals.

The more we damage the world, the less able it becomes

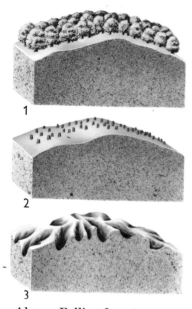

Above: Felling forests can destroy soil:
(1) Forest trees nourish soil and their roots bind it. (2) If trees are felled soil loses nourishment and strength. (3) When it rains the bare soil is washed away.

Left: Re-using scrap from dumps like this makes metals last longer.

to produce enough to satisfy our needs. Soon, too, we may use up certain minerals and fossil fuels that we depend on for our energy supply.

Nations might go to war to fight over what is left. If they fight with nuclear bombs everyone and most other living things could die.

Saving the Earth

Mankind can still do many things to save the Earth's surface from damage.

Setting land aside as nature parks helps preserve wild animals and plants. Careful farming and forestry keep soil nourished well enough to go on growing crops and trees. Laws against pollution help to clear poisons from the air and water.

But worldwide hunger, poverty and war remain risks unless we eat less wastefully and use less of scarce fossil fuels and minerals.

Raising more plants and fewer animals would yield extra food. Re-using scrap metal and using energy from wind and waves would help save fossil fuels. But the main need is to reduce the human population.

Above: Spilt oil at sea kills countless seabirds.

Right: A nuclear bomb. Such bombs could kill every living thing on Earth.

Surprising Facts

Natural Wonders

Height in metres

500
400
300
200
100

The three places described on these two pages would deserve a place in any list of the greatest natural wonders of the world.

A Mushroom Mountain
One day in 1943 smoke rose from a field in western Mexico. A farmer working in the field was scared and ran.

Hours later, the ground gaped apart and hot cinders forced their way out through the hole. After a day they had formed a house-high hillock. In a week this grew into a mound 150 metres high. After a year a cinder mountain had swallowed up the field and nearby lands.

People named the volcano Paricutín, after a nearby village. Even this was doomed as the volcano grew. It spewed ash that smothered Paricutín village. Then it poured lava that flowed five kilometres and drowned another village. Two years after it emerged, Mount Paricutín stood 500 metres high.

Rainbow Bridge
Rainbow Bridge in southern Utah was made not by people but by nature. It stretches 85 metres across a gorge 94 metres deep.

Long ago, a looping river cut caves in opposite sides of a cliff top. Both caves met and the cliff top overhead became a bridge no more than 6·7 metres wide.

This may be the largest natural arch, although Landscape Arch in Utah is longer..

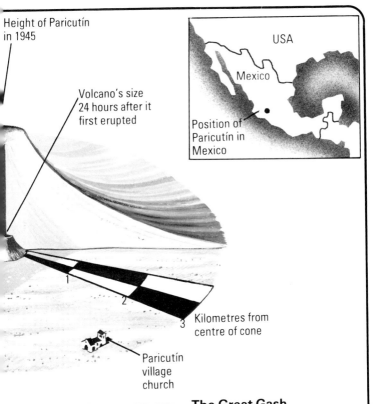

Height of Paricutín in 1945

Volcano's size 24 hours after it first erupted

USA

Mexico

Position of Paricutín in Mexico

1

2

3 Kilometres from centre of cone

Paricutín village church

The Great Gash

The Grand Canyon in north-west Arizona is the world's largest gorge. It stretches almost 500 kilometres. In places it is 20 kilometres wide and more than two kilometres deep.

The canyon was formed by the Colorado River, which deepened its bed as fast as the land around it rose. The layered rocks of the gorge show more of the Earth's past than any other place.

Exploring the World

It took thousands of years for Stone Age peoples to spread around the world. Today, artificial satellites in space can scan our planet in seconds.

Stone Age Seafarers

Three thousand years ago Stone Age farmers in South-East Asia began sailing off to seek new homes on the islands of the Pacific Ocean. Families went by canoe or by catamaran—a platform lashed across two canoes (inset). From such early craft came the outrigger—a canoe balanced by a log fixed out from one side (below).

Birds, clouds, stars and ocean currents helped guide them across the ocean. In time these Stone Age adventurers settled many of the far-flung islands that we now call Polynesia.

Spy in the Sky

People first mapped the world by measuring its surface from the ground. This task took centuries. Now cameras in orbiting satellites can photograph the Earth in minutes.

Landsats like the one shown here have orbited the Earth from pole to pole. Their cameras have taken films that show up things invisible to human eyes. Such satellites help to map lands which are too wild to explore easily. They show where crops are damaged by disease, and where poisons are polluting air or water. They even help geologists to find new mineral deposits.

Catamaran

Freak Weather

Changing weather brings us cloud, sunshine, wind and rain. Sometimes, unusual weather conditions produce effects so strange that they are almost unbelievable.

Seeing Things!

A layer of 'thick' cold air or of 'thin' hot air near the ground bends light rays and produces the effects known as mirages.

In hot, sunny deserts, a layer of hot air forms just above the ground. If your eye is just above the level of this layer, the light from distant clouds may hit the layer and bounce up to your eye. So you seem to see the clouds upside down, lying like pools of water on the ground.

You get a similar effect when hot air forms above a road. The sky appears like pools of water lying on the road surface.

Effects like these are called *inferior* mirages.

In polar climates a layer of cold air may also form above the ground. Light from the

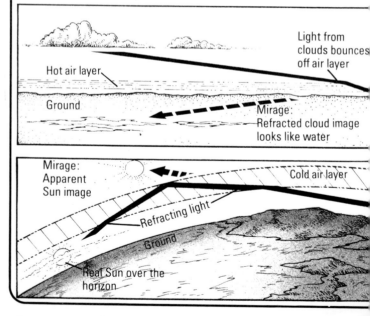

Light from clouds bounces off air layer

Hot air layer

Ground

Mirage: Refracted cloud image looks like water

Mirage: Apparent Sun image

Cold air layer

Refracting light

Ground

Real Sun over the horizon

Sun, which may be far over the horizon, bends downward where it passes through this layer.

So if you are looking through a cold-air layer you seem to see the Sun positioned high in the sky, far from its true position.

This kind of effect is called a *superior* mirage.

Strange Sunsets

In 1883 the Indonesian volcano Krakatoa exploded, and affected the atmosphere in strange ways. So much ash was hurled into the air that it blotted out the Sun and darkness lasted for two days

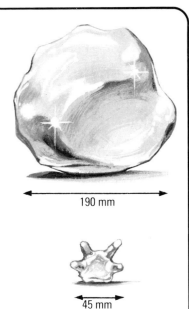

190 mm

45 mm

INFERIOR MIRAGE

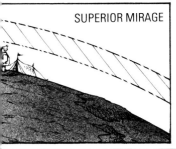

SUPERIOR MIRAGE

at places up to 80 kilometres from Krakatoa.

Volcanic dust flung high into the sky caused bright red sunsets all around the world for years to follow.

Bombed by Ice

Hailstones are balls of ice that fall in storms. Most are no bigger than peas. But some are huge. The giant hailstone shown above weighed 750 grammes. It fell in the United States in 1970. The strangely shaped hailstone below it fell in Australia in 1971. Hailstones can ruin crops. Large ones even smash glass roofs.

Lost Lands

In places, rising sea has drowned the land. In other places, sea will drown the land if not prevented.

The Bering Bridge

Today, a narrow neck of sea cuts off North America from Asia. But Stone Age families reached North America by simply walking there from Asia. They could do this because ice sheets held so much of the world's water that the ocean level fell by as much as 90 metres. An isthmus then linked Asia and North America. Geographers call that vanished corridor of land the Bering Land Bridge.

Atlantis

Over two thousand years ago Greek legends told of Atlantis—an island empire drowned by earthquakes. In the 1960s, archaeologists found remains of an ancient city buried by volcanic ash on the small Greek island of Thíra. This had been part of

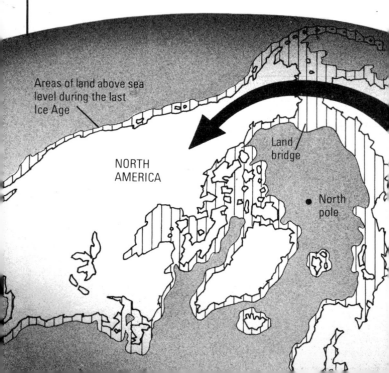

Areas of land above sea level during the last Ice Age

NORTH AMERICA

Land bridge

North pole

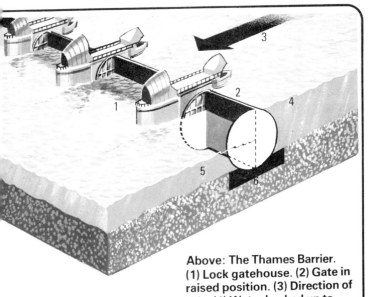

**Above: The Thames Barrier.
(1) Lock gatehouse. (2) Gate in
raised position. (3) Direction of
tide. (4) Water backed up to
gate. (5) Low water behind
gate. (6) Foundation of gate.**

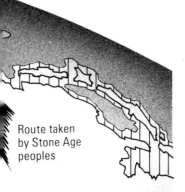

Route taken
by Stone Age
peoples

ASIA

Santorini, a larger island that
blew up in a huge volcanic
explosion some 3400 years
ago. Santorini may have
been Atlantis.

Sinking Cities

London is slowly sinking in
the clay it stands on. One
day the River Thames could
overflow and drown low-
lying land. To stop this,
engineers have built huge
flood gates across the river.
If an extra high tide moves
up-river from the sea, the
gates will shut it out.

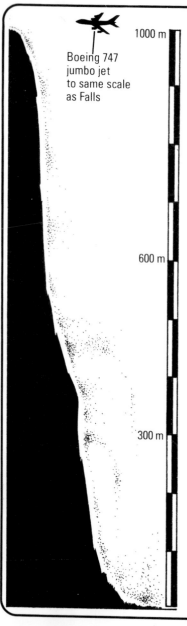

Boeing 747
jumbo jet
to same scale
as Falls

1000 m

600 m

300 m

Freshwater Wonders

Less than one per cent of the world's water is fresh water yet its effects are quite remarkable.

Angel Falls

In 1935 an American airman was flying through a gorge in a Venezuelan plateau. Suddenly he glimpsed a narrow river plunging over a cliff. Its waters fell in an almost straight line.

From top to bottom the full waterfall measured 979

Left: Angel Falls would dwarf a jumbo jet. The map shows their position.

Venezuela — Angel Falls

SOUTH AMERICA

metres. It proved to be the highest in the world. Geographers called it Angel Falls after James Angel, the airman who discovered it.

China's Sorrow

This is an apt nickname for China's Hwang Ho. This river's flooding has killed more people than any other natural disaster. Much of the river flows between banks higher than the plain around. Heavy rains can make it burst its banks and swamp huge areas. In 1931 a flood like the one shown above drowned nearly four million people. Such floods can shift the river's course, and move its mouth hundreds of kilometres.

Vanished Lakes

Most lakes dry up in time. Many fill with mud; others simply leak away. One that vanished like this was Lake Agassiz in North America. This vast lake was almost as big as New Zealand. It filled a hollow rimmed by mountains and a mighty ice sheet. When the ice melted most of the lake escaped.

But parts of it remain. They now form smaller lakes including lakes Winnipeg, Winnipegosis and Manitoba.

Ocean Wonders

People have mapped the oceans and their floors. Yet there is always something in the sea to startle and amaze us.

Mighty Midgets

Just below the sea a broken wall of coral stretches 2000 kilometres off the coast of north-east Australia. A hole drilled into Eniwetok Atoll— an island in the Pacific Ocean —penetrated coral up to 1400 metres deep.

Yet these vast amounts of coral are mostly made of tiny coral cups, each no bigger than a tooth. The builders of these billions of cups are coral polyps, little relatives of sea anemones. Each forms a hard cup to guard its soft body.

A Disappearing Sea

In 1970 scientists found thick salt deposits beneath the Mediterranean Sea. Such

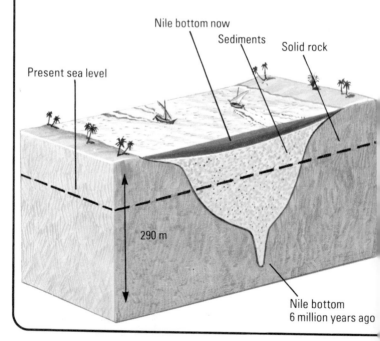

Nile bottom now

Sediments

Solid rock

Present sea level

290 m

Nile bottom
6 million years ago

deposits originate on desert shores, so scientists suspected that the Mediterranean had once been far lower and smaller than it is now.

Meanwhile other scientists learnt that a deep rocky gorge lay 290 metres below the soft muddy floor of the River Nile. Long ago the Nile must have reached the Mediterranean by flowing along that gorge. This proves that the sea itself once lay over 290 metres lower than today.

Scientists think it almost dried up because Africa met Spain and stopped water flowing into the Mediterranean from the Atlantic Ocean. If this happened again the Mediterranean could dry up in 1000 years.

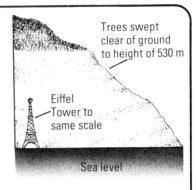

Trees swept clear of ground to height of 530 m

Eiffel Tower to same scale

Sea level

The Greatest Wave
In 1958, 90 million tonnes of rock slid 900 metres into Alaska's Lituya Bay.

This rock fall unleashed a wave 530 metres high—twice as high as France's famous Eiffel Tower. As the illustration above shows, the wave tore out ten square kilometres of forest and soil, exposing barren rock.

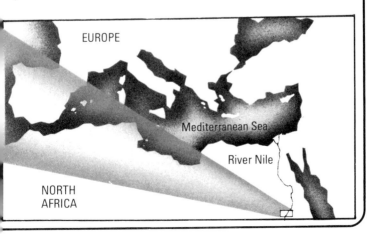

EUROPE

Mediterranean Sea

River Nile

NORTH AFRICA

Wandering Plants and Animals

Mountains, deserts, oceans and other barriers stop the spread of many plants and animals. Yet living things have reached and colonized the remotest islands.

Amazing Monarchs
Millions of monarch butterflies migrate north and south each year in North America. Some get blown far out to sea.

Summer range

Winter range

The left-hand map shows that these fragile insects have island-hopped thousands of kilometres west across the Pacific Ocean, reaching Australia, Indonesia, and even southern China.

The other map shows that monarchs driven eastward on Atlantic Ocean winds can reach the British Isles, and the Canary Islands off northwest Africa.

Floating Zoos

Sometimes plants and animals are washed far out to sea on rafts of vegetation torn loose from river banks by floods. Once, a ship's captain glimpsed a monkey or a squirrel leaping from tree to tree on a floating island in the sea off South-East Asia. A man who fell asleep beside the River Congo woke up on a floating island far out in the Atlantic Ocean.

Most such accidental travellers just drown. But a few land on remote oceanic islands. This is how lizards and tortoises reached the Galápagos Islands, 1000 kilometres west of mainland South America. Almost all of Madagascar's land animals floated in from Africa.

Coconut Colonists

A few land plants actually use the sea to help them spread. Coconut palms drop coconuts that fall into the sea. Ocean currents can carry coconuts hundreds of kilometres. Some sprout when they have been washed up on lonely island shores.

Tomorrow's World

Between them, mankind and nature may make tomorrow's world very different from the world we know today.

Man and the Sea

One day tugs may tow huge Antarctic icebergs all the way to sunny California (below). Enough ice would survive the trip to provide huge supplies of cheap fresh water.

People might do much more. Engineers have plans to close the Mediterranean Sea, and separate the Arctic Ocean from the Pacific.

If Ice Sheets Melt

If the world's great ice sheets melted, the level of the sea could rise by 90 metres. This would be enough to drown all the planet's seaports and many of its major cities.

For instance, in the United States, all of Florida would disappear.

But if a new ice age dawned, the level of the sea would fall, exposing vast new tracts of land. Some scientists expect another ice age to begin at almost any time.

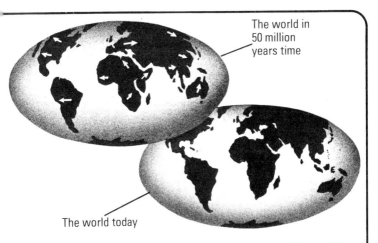

The world in 50 million years time

The world today

Fifty Million Years On

For more than 50 million years Africa and South America have moved apart by four centimetres a year. The continents will continue to drift apart. Fifty million years on, the Americas may have moved far west; Australia may have ridden over Indonesia; Africa may have split apart.

Index

Page numbers in *italics* refer to illustrations